JIM LARSSON

HOW TO BECOME
A COACH
AND BUILD A THRIVING
PRACTICE

Contents

1   Introduction

Coaching is one of the fastest growing industries in the world. Everyday new coaches enter the market. Schools, institutes and academies offer coach training programs and consultancy firms quickly add coaching and offer it to their clients as one of their new key services.

There is a reason for this. Apparently coaching is booming because of the results and the tremendous value that is to be gained by being coached. The majority of full-time coaches around the world have not received formal coach training and are not certified by any governing body. Does this mean that they are not great coaches? No, of course not. They became great coaches because they get results. And how did they do that?

1.1   Characteristics of a GREAT coach…

- Great coaches generally don't have huge egos
- Great coaches are excellent listeners, and not just everyday listening, but listening at a deep level • Great coaches ask great questions and they know when to ask them.
- Great coaches love life and love coaching
- Great coaches see potential in their coachees and then hold onto that potential and do whatever they can to encourage their coachee to reach it
- Great coaches are responsible for their lives – they know that they have the power and the choices to create the sort of life they want to live
- Great coaches are non-judgmental. They understand their job and they know that their coachees know what is best for them.

Great coaches really care about their coachees. And by empowering them, they empower themselves and the world in general. I firmly believe that when people around the globe start embracing a more coaching approach as a new way of interacting with others, the world would become a much nicer place to live in.

Today there are multiple ways to become a professional coach. You can enroll in a coach training program, get certified and start running your own coaching practice. Every coach training facilitator will tell you that it's almost a 'no brainer' to start a thriving coaching practice. Well, here's a news flash, it's just not that easy. It's not enough to be a great coach, you have to be a great entrepreneur as well. You're running a business.

But when you are considering coaching as a new career, you want to know more about it and would like to find out if it 'is for you', this course will give you all you need to know and more.

This is a great place to start.

Learn all about coaching with this "How to become a coach" e-course.

This book gives you the answers on how to pave your way to become a successful coach, guiding people to happier and more triumphant lives.

Have fun reading it and when you're finished…start coaching. The world needs you!

I hope to salute you one day as one of my fellow coaching practitioners. Feel free to stay in touch with me!

Cheers,

Ton de Graaf

2   A Brief History of Coaching

All coaching is, taking a player where he can't take himself

Bill McCartney

Coaching has its roots in the area of sports, of
course, and, as such, dates back at least as far as
ancient Greece where well-paid coaches trained
many of the athletes competing in the original Olympic games

Carpenter, 2004

As it applies to the workplace, however, coaching is a much more recent development. There has been individualized training in the form of apprenticeships for hundreds of years, but the earliest form of such coaching as we know it today was called "developmental counseling". From 1940 to 1979, coaching tended to be performed by organization consultants. During this initial period, coaches were primarily psychologists and organization development (OD) professionals who were focused on OD issues. There was often an informal aspect to it. For example, an executive coach who remembers this period recalls a CEO stopping her in a hallway and asking if she could stop by and chat for an hour or two.

From 1980 to 1994, the field of coaching experienced rapid growth, quickly expanding into many new areas of service (personal coaching, outplacement, career coaching, etc.).

Our field was accelerated by complexities associated with increased downsizing, mergers, acquisitions, and outplacement. The leader's role evolved to deal with rising levels of ambiguity and pressures to perform in an increasingly global context. Top managers were asked to be both strategic decision makers and masters of the "soft" skills required to effectively manage people.

From 1995 to the present, the amount of executive and workforce coaching has continued to grow. There has been an increase in the number of publications devoted to coaching, in organizations that offer training to coaches, in the establishment of coaching organizations, and in the focus placed on coaching research by academia. Because the field is wide open to anyone who wants to enter, it is difficult to know the exact number of people performing coaching services.

Today's coaches come from variety of backgrounds and professions, including business, law, teaching, psychology, therapy, human resources, and sports and they don't necessarily join coaching organizations.

3   The Purposes of Coaching

According to the literature, leadership development is often viewed as the purpose of most coaching assignments. Organizations also employ coaches to help with leader transitions (such as promotions, lateral moves, or international assignments), to retain high potentials, to improve performance that is off track, and to help individuals assess where their career is now and where it may go next. Some coaching focuses on honing specific business skills. For example, one company helps leaders learn to be more productive by giving them coaching on improving their organizational skills. Coaching is tied to training programs in some companies. For example, a manager attends training for some specified number of hours and then gets individual coaching to reinforce and apply things learned in the workshop.

There is also "Personal coaching," which helps clients set and achieve goals in aspects of their lives other than just business. Personal coaching is usually funded by the individual.

3.1   Personal Coaching is not new.

Coaching is a thought provoking, structured process that assists people and or teams to perform at the peak of their ability, achieving goals faster, with increased clarity and purpose.

In Middle English the word 'coche' meant "a wagon or carriage", with the literal translation of 'coach' being a vehicle taking a person or group of people from one location to a desired destination.

Even though it's value is becoming more and more widely acknowledged, it is interesting to hear how people have different ideas about what coaching exactly constitutes. Many people seem to link coaching to counseling or performance management and think if they have coaching is about fixing their problems rather than enhancing their potential. Like sports coaching people get that it's about reaching goals, but still sometimes they don't translate how this could work for them in their professional or private life.

A major consideration for many people is how or why they should consider coaching. One interesting trend, you may or may not be aware of, is that many highly successful corporations or organizations have already established coaching programs as a means of rewarding and enhancing their organizational growth. These organizations recognize the long term benefits of support and developing their most important resource, their people, particularly high performers. High performing employees as well as emerging leaders and middle managers now more often than not are encouraged to consider one on one coaching. This in turn generates organizational success, builds internal feelings of respect, motivation and value.

Executive coaching covers career transition, project and performance coaching. Project coaching is more about empowering strategic management of teams to achieve the most effective results they can; performance coaching focuses on enhancing potential in a specific context and transitional coaching centered on career changes and opportunities.

Personal coaching on the other hand is another fast growing option people consider to reach their personal goals and desires faster than they would otherwise. Like transitional coaching, Personal coaching is designed to help people effectively manage a variety of performance areas experienced, but in their personal life. As an Executive Coach it is not uncommon to cross into this area of coaching while at the same time working on career or leadership goals.

So, for arguments sake, let's keep it clear and simple: our emerging profession can be divided into three main areas; Sports, Personal and Business coaching. In this book I focus on the latter two. Sports coaching is very much different from the other area's because of the nature of the coaching process. A sports coach tells his players what to do and then they do it. A Personal or Business coach never tell their coachees what to do. That would be taking over the responsibility for the happiness and purposeful living of their coachees. That's dis-empowering since it only teaches the coachees that they can't do it themselves, they need help form a professional coach. Coaches are not better than their coachees, they don't have all the right answers. Great coaches know that the coachee already has the answers inside of them. Great coaches believe in the strengths, creativity and resourcefulness of their coachees. Their job is it to facilitate and perhaps speed up that process.

Whether it is Business or Personal coaching, each is tailored to help people on a number of different levels. The sort of issues covered include identity, values, beliefs, behaviors as well as competencies.

Organizations need to ask themselves, how can we effectively measure and track our coaching programs so as to best meet our future organizational growth, demands and impacts? Individuals on the other hand may ask…is coaching what I need right now, and if so how can I maximize the experience and with whom?

4   What is coaching all about?

The **International Coaching Federation**, defines coaching in the following way:

> *Coaching is partnering with clients in a thought-provoking and creative process that inspires them to maximize their personal and professional potential.*

> *Professional coaches provide an ongoing partnership designed to help clients produce fulfilling results in their personal and professional lives. Coaches help people improve their performances and enhance the quality of their lives.*

> *Coaches are trained to listen, to observe and to customize their approach to individual client needs. They seek to elicit solutions and strategies from the client; they believe the client is naturally creative and resourceful. The coach's job is to provide support to enhance the skills, resources, and creativity that the client already has.*

The **Worldwide Association of Business Coaches** (WABC) is an international professional association of qualified business coaches who work with businesses, organizations and governments. Here's how they define business coaching.

Reprinted with permission of the Worldwide Association of *Business Coaches*.

4.1   WABC Business Coaching Definition

> *Business coaching is the process of engaging in meaningful communication with individuals in businesses, organizations, institutions or governments, with the goal of promoting success at all levels of the organization by affecting the actions of those individuals.*

> *Business coaching enables the client to understand and enhance his or her role in achieving business success. The*

business coach helps the client discover how personal characteristics, including a sense of self and personal perspectives, affect personal and business processes and the ability to reach objectives within a business context. With this method, successful coaching helps the client learn how to change or accommodate personal characteristics and how to create personal and business processes that achieve objectives.

Business coaching establishes an atmosphere of trust, respect, safety, challenge and accountability to motivate both the coach and the client. In turn, this requires that the business coach conduct an ethical and competent practice, based on appropriate professional experience and business knowledge and an understanding of individual and organizational change.

Coaching is strongest in the United States, followed by the United Kingdom, Japan, Canada, Australia, Singapore, Europe and New Zealand, and is reaching more and more countries all the time.

Coaching still is an emerging profession. It combines the best concepts from business, psychology, philosophy, sports and spirituality. Although coaching combines skills from other disciplines, it is a distinct process of supporting others to create an ideal life.

Coaches work with clients on a variety of topics: from business and professional issues to personal and spiritual concerns. A coach is an advocate, a sounding board, a cheerleader, an accountability partner, a truth teller and a supporter.

Coaching involves a professional partnership between a coach and the coachee. Coaches listen to their coachee's problems or concerns, and then provide coaching through which the coachee determines what steps to take to overcome his or her problems and move ahead.

The definition of coaching is still very much a subject for many discussions in the coaching community. Stay in touch with the leading associations (like WABC) to stay informed and involved in the development of our wonderful profession.

5   What Coaching is not

As an emerging profession, coaching draws on a range of other more traditional professions including psychology, business consulting, mentoring, management theory and adult learning. However, coaching is a unique field and there are significant differences between coaching and these fields.

5.1   Coaching and Therapy

Coaching is not therapy, counseling or psychology. Although intervention often follows some psychological models such as behavioral theory, the actual process of coaching is quite different from a therapeutic intervention.

One of the most obvious differences between the two approaches is that therapy tends to focus on feelings and experiences related to past events, whereas coaching is oriented towards goal setting and encourages the client to move forward.

A therapist typically works with a dysfunctional person to get them to become functional. A coach works with a functional person to get them to become exceptional. Therapists typically work with people who need help to become emotionally healthy. A coach works with people who are already emotionally healthy to move them to magnificent levels.

Coaching does not rely on past issues for achieving growth, but rather focuses on goals towards the future. Coaching is action and future oriented. You can analyze the past as much as you want, you won't change that, nor will it change today or tomorrow. The focus is on where the coachee is right now, where they want to be next, and how to get there.

If you are working with the past, then you are involved in therapy. If the coachee is stuck and can't seem to move forward or if there is a drug or alcohol problem, then you are more likely doing something other than coaching. Often starting a coaching process will help a coachee realize a need for therapy. Be alert. If you feel uncomfortable or uneasy about where the conversation is leading, tell your coachee. Part of being a good coach is knowing when and when not to coach. If the coachee needs therapy then refer them to a therapist. It is the ethical way to go.

5.2   Homework

5.2.1   Referring a client to a therapist

Barbara is an area sales manager for a chain of toy stores, a position she has held for 8 years. Her primary role at work is to lead a team of store managers and to analyze sales trends and develop specific sales goals and campaigns. Barbara is very good at what she does, but has one major weakness; while excellent at communicating with individuals or small groups, she is very poor when it comes to giving presentations to large groups.

Barbara engages a Personal Coach, Steve, to help her with the specific issue of public speaking. In their first meeting, Barbara is able to articulate a strong desire to move to the national sales management team. She talks about her love of her job, the company and its vision and the joy she gets from developing successful sales campaigns. Steve supports Barbara in her belief that a move to the national sales management team is a worthy and achievable goal. When they begin to talk about the specific issue of public speaking, however, Barbara becomes visibly anxious and despairs of ever being able to overcome her problem.

When they meet for the second time, Steve begins to ask Barbara about her history of public speaking. Without saying anything, Barbara bursts into tears. Steve sits patiently for some time until Barbara is able to compose herself to speak. Barbara tells him about her immense distress at having to give presentations at work. She tells him that whenever she has to give a presentation she spends night after night on the PowerPoint slides. She feels sick in the stomach and unable to sleep for days before hand. Moments before she has to present, her anxiety is often so high that she feels like she could pass out. Steve asks Barbara if she is willing to go through a visualization exercise with him, but Barbara explains that she feels too emotionally drained to continue and they finish up.

When they next meet, Barbara tells Steve that she has had a tumultuous week and has had to take a few days off because she has been too emotionally overwrought to work. Barbara tells him that she believes that her fear of public speaking results from a trauma, something that happened when she was a teenager, that she hadn't thought about clearly until now. Barbara also tells Steve that she doesn't want to tell him what it is, because it is too painful.

Coach:	Can I give you some feedback Barbara?
Barbara:	(still obviously distressed nods her head)
Coach:	First I want to tell you how brave I think you are coming to see me today. You are obviously deeply distressed about public speaking. The easiest thing to do would be to run away and hide but you have chosen to face the problem head on and I applaud you for that. The past week must have been very hard for you.
Barbara:	It was. I hate missing work. It feels as though I've made the problem worse. I can't really see a way out?
Coach:	Barbara, I would suggest that you consider seeing a counselor or therapist. What I'm seeing is a very capable and confident person with one major stumbling block, standing in the way of even more success in your life. If you believe that there is a link between public speaking and the past trauma, then I think exploring that someone qualified to help you, would be well worth doing.
Barbara:	You might be right. I don't feel as though I'm capable of being coached right now. I'm just too upset.
Coach:	That's fine. You can always come back to coaching at a later date if you want. Do you know of any good therapists?
Barbara:	Not really. Although a friend of mine is seeing one and there's one that does work for our HR department. I've never thought much about it.
Coach:	Can I make a suggestion?
Barbara:	Sure.
Coach:	I'd like to suggest that we commit to two more sessions with a goal of finding the right therapist for you. I'd like you to do some homework finding out about the two therapists that you mentioned, the one that your friend sees and the woman from the HR department and I will email you some information about what to look for in a therapist. What do you think of that suggestion?
Barbara:	OK. I would appreciate some help.

Questions

- Do you support Steve's decision to not continue with coaching until Barbara has sought the help of a professional therapist?
- Would you have handled this situation differently to Steve? How?

Let us assume that Barbara's therapy is successful in helping her cope with her trauma from the past to the point where she feels ready to work with a coach again. If you were her new coach, what techniques and tools would you use to assist Barbara to improve her public speaking?

5.3   Coaching and consulting

Coaching is often seen as consulting. However, there are distinct differences between these disciplines.

A consultant is usually a specialist in a given area. A consultant is hired to give recommendations and provide solutions. A consultant works with a client to solve a particular problem or to address a specific issue. Once the problem is solved or the issue addressed, the consultant leaves.

Generally, a consultant doesn't get involved with areas outside of their specialty.

Coaching uses a more holistic approach. With the coachee, the coach examines the situation, creates a plan of action, and works side by side to resolve the issue. The coach does not have to be an expert in the coachee's business. The coachee is the expert. The coach collaborates with the coachee to create a solution using the coachee's knowledge and answers.

While people, and companies, will often choose a coach who has previous experience or expertise in the field that they work in, coaching does not require this.

Consultants however, build their businesses around the knowledge they have gathered over time in the specific field in which they then offer consulting expertise. They are expected to provide advice, information and anecdotes about the field. The coach, on the other hand, does not have the answers and does not claim to have them. They ask questions that allow the coachee to find their own answers and clarify their own values.

5.4   Coaching and mentoring

The term "mentoring" originates from Homer's Odyssey. In the Odyssey, the character Mentor advises, supports and counsels Telemachus, Odysseus' son as Telemachus prepares to take on the responsibilities of the family in his father's absence. Mentor also advises Odysseus on how to search for his father. Telemachus thanks him for his help: "Sir, I thank you for your kindness; you might be a father speaking to his own son, and I will not forget one word of what you say…"

The mentor is usually older and more experienced than the person being mentored. The mentor bestows his knowledge and wisdom onto the student. The student looks up to the mentor and seeks guidance and advice from the mentor. There are both formal and informal mentoring relationships.

In a business setting, mentoring is a formal relationship that is established with someone who is an expert in his or her field. Like consulting, mentoring involves passing on the benefit of a set of specific experiences. A coaching relationship, on the other hand, is a partnership whereby the coach walks side by side with the coachee. The coach supports the coachee in drawing on their own wisdom and following their inner guidance.

5.5   What is the difference between an Executive, Corporate or SME Coach?

The coachee is the distinguishing feature of the above coaches. Executive coaches work with executives, usually senior executives in medium to larger sized companies. They tend to be employed by either the executive themselves or the company. Either way they are most often brought in to coach on performance related or life-work balance issues and they most often take the role of strategic partner to the client.

Corporate coaches also work with executives, usually in medium to larger sized companies. However they tend to be employed more often by the company and coach on company defined goals and targets. They also take the role of strategic partner to the coachee. SME coaches can work with small business owners, entrepreneurs and managers of business units in companies.

Depending on the coachee their role could be anything from life-work balance to specific business building goals (for example, to increase sales by 30%).

Generally speaking corporate, SME and executive coaches will have expertise in their area of coaching. SME coaches will have run a small business, executive coaches have often been CEO's or senior executives themselves. Although the coaching methodology does not demand this, there are two key reasons why it occurs:

1. It helps to have an empathy or understanding of where the client is coming from, particularly in relation to culture and language. A corporate coach who has never heard of key performance indicators, or doesn't know the elements of a strategic plan will be more challenged.
2. The second and main reason has to do with marketing. There is a saying in the coaching profession that all coaching is Personal coaching after the first 3 sessions. You may have been brought in to double sales, but you will find that very quickly the sessions become about relationships, communication, family-work balance and doubling sales.

So it is possible that a powerful Personal coach would do a great job at coaching a senior executive. In fact it is probably what he or she needs. But from a marketing perspective CEO's of companies like to employ people who have come from that culture. Likewise small business owners like to know that their coach understands what it is to run a small business.

Coaches do not give advice, nor do they offer therapy. They simply act like a facilitator to help people achieve individual goals. Through Personal Coaching people live a better life as they get help in making the right moves, which they are not able to make on their own. This does not mean that no one can work out things on their own. It rather means the opposite.

Everyone has some limitations, which directly or indirectly affect a number of areas in his or her life or how he or she looks at different situations in life. These limitations or challenges, whether mental, emotional or psychological, create barriers and hold up personal development.

This is when a Personal Coach comes in. The process of coaching helps people break those barriers themselves and pave the way to achieving their goals.

A number of people correlate the work of a Personal Coach to that of a psychologist. That's not the same. While a psychologist focuses on analyzing your past actions and getting to the root of the problem, a Personal Coach concentrates on helping you to frame the right steps in future to achieve your individual goal.

A psychologist might offer therapy and advice. A Personal Coach never does.

A very good analogy is that of a Fitness Trainer.

Consider you are joining a gym. Your fitness trainer will first ask you what you want to achieve. Whether you want to

Lose weight?
Lose fat?
Build muscles? Build
endurance? Increase
stamina?

The trainer will then see where you stand now in relation to your goal.

For example, if you want to trim down body fat, you will be asked to take a body fat composition test to measure the current body fat level. You may have to take a fitness test and may be asked about present eating habits. All this is a part of helping you get nearer to your goal.

The fitness trainer will first establish standards for you as to how much fat you intend to lose and over what period of time. It is based on all this that he designs a plan of action for you to reach your goal.

Having done this, he also supplies you with the required backing and support in the form of constant encouragement and motivation.

There may be many people who look towards reducing weight. But what they lack is the willpower and confidence to keep it up.

The trainer's job is to guide them through the dificult path towards their goal. He has to help the people achieve their goals more quickly and more effectively than if they tried by themselves.

This is what a Personal Coach also does for you.

Here's a real life example.

Jane and Bill were married and leading a happy life together. Both of them were employed. Bill was not very content with his job. He was looking for better opportunities, and as it just had to be, he got an offer from an overseas firm. The position was just what he wanted. It was time for him to take a decision.

If he took the job he would be happy career-wise but staying separate lives, would their marriage survive? He could not possibly be selfish to ask Jane to leave her job. And if he let go of the new job offer, he would feel guilty of having given up a great chance. Now this is what we call a fix!

What would you do if you were in Bill's place? Very dificult to decide, isn't it?

A Personal Coach enters a person's life to help him live it better. Every person has problems. It may be a lack of confidence for someone, weak communication skills for another, or a lost career for someone else or even a problem with relationships.

The areas that a coach can work on are:

Confidence and Self-esteem
- Feel good about yourself
- Have no room for self-doubt
- Get to know new people and be confident •
Speak confidently in front of groups

Career

- Know which job is right for you •

Move on to a better job

- Perform better on the job •

Earn a promotion

- Start your own business •

Excel as a leader

Relationships
- Be a good listener
- Work through problems with your partner •
Sail smoothly through tough times
- Build stronger bonds

Communication
- How to communicate with anyone? •
Talking to strangers
- How to get your point across effectively?

Health / losing weight
- Improve your health •
Reduce stress
- Follow a healthy eating pattern •
Sticking to an exercise plan

Dreams and achievement •
Set firm goals
- Work out what you want from life •
Provide direction and purpose
- Have more fun
- Have more energy and always be ready for more

Money/Finance
- Earn more money •
  Save more money
- Work out budgets and follow them

Getting what you want in life
- Becoming more organized
- Getting rid of barriers and negative thinking •
Manage your time more effectively
- Discover your values in life
- Clear the clutter that you are engulfed in •
How to stay focused

It covers almost everything that life is about as you might have noticed.

6   The Role of a Personal Coach

A Personal Coach doesn't spoon-feed; he facilitates. He is a guide, a medium to finding solutions. He is a motivational figure who coaches a coachee towards winning ultimate success.

A Personal Coach challenges, questions and nudges a person forward so that all inner potential can be unlocked.

Anytime in life, when you feel that you are trudging on pointlessly, Personal Coaching will help you sit back and analyze what went wrong and where you need to make amendments.

Personal Coaching, in that sense, provides a coachee with self-awareness, focus and accountability.

A Personal Coach is a comrade, a shoulder to cry on, a guide, a philosopher, a parasol on a rainy day, a lifeboat and a cheerleader. He or she helps to make choices, polishes communication skills, and most significantly acts as a road map to finding all that a coachee wanted in his or her life. The coachee, however, sits in the driver's seat and determines the direction. The coach sits in the passenger's seat making sure the coachee knows exactly where he or she is going.

A point to remember is a Personal Coach does not promise that his or her client will fulfill dreams and achieve whatever he or she wants to.

7   How Does Coaching Work?

Personal Coaching is a matter of choice, which once made can lead to improving life skills. Now is when the question arises- how does coaching work?

There are several ways to get coaching started.

1–2–1 sessions in person
1–2–1 sessions on the telephone 1–
2–1 sessions using email
Group coaching sessions in person
Group coaching via the telephone (teleclass)

No matter what method is used the approach is the same.

There is no doubt that telephone, email and group sessions will work as effectively as a life session. Whatever be the medium, all sessions will be equally effectual in recognizing the coachee's aims, challenges, plans and thoughts, and possibly assign fieldwork that will get him going and bring him closer to all that he has always dreamed of achieving.

Fieldwork isn't like the homework you were assigned in school. It consists of action steps to move you closer toward your goals and dreams. The coachee brings the agenda and the coach brings the coaching skills to create a partnership that moves the client forward.

The client calls the coach at a scheduled time each week.

7.1   One-on-one Coaching

There is no strict pattern to Personal Coaching. In fact, a coach will schedule one that is tailor-made for the coachee.

The basic design consists of:

- A complementary "Is this for you?" session lasting around 30–45 minutes
- An over-the-phone or in-person one-hour session to develop the foundation of a coaching strategy
- A preliminary assessment to gauge work and personal needs and determine goals • Continuous, regular coaching sessions over phone or email
- Developing self-awareness, promoting creative thinking and building up practical skills with exercises
- Execution of sessions in full confidentiality
- Quarterly evaluation, and review of strategies for constant backing and to meet new requirements

Coaching sessions are usually scheduled weekly, lasting from a half-hour to two hours. The length and frequency of sessions can vary to suit the coachee's purpose and convenience.

Sessions may be focused on one specific goal or challenge that the coachee is facing, or on a much broader set of personal or professional issues.

7.2   Group coaching

The one-to-one coaching programs can be easily applied to group coaching sessions too. This is the most cost-effective model for providing coaching throughout an organization. Coaching groups is about the interaction process, how do team members communicate with each other, or with other teams, and how does this help achieving the defined team results. A team coach focuses on the process and not on the content. What does a team need to become a more mature and effective team. A coach can guide a team through the different phases of growth and leverage, speed up, the process.

This was in a nutshell what coaching is and what it involves. Here's a small exercise to check whether you got the key points down.

7.3   Homework

7.3.1   Do you want to become a coach?

There are a few questions you should answer, and sort out your thoughts and plans before you take the plunge. Here's how…

In readiness for next session I'd like you to:

- Write down WHY you are thinking of becoming a Personal Coach.
- List the key skills that you think are required to be an outstanding coach. Not just a good coach, but an OUTSTANDING coach. Have you been coached yourself? Have you seen any great coaches in action? If so, what do they do?
- Have a look over the material in this session again – especially the list that details some of the most popular reasons why people come to a coach – ask yourself – "Without any formal training, could I help people who come to me with this problem? What life experience have I had in this field?" Go down each and give yourself a rating of 1–10, with a 10 being you are an expert and could help this person without any training or further help.

7.3.2   Do you have what it takes?

It is time to tread on more crucial grounds. Now that you know what coaching concerns, you might be closer to understanding if coaching is a career for you.

But there's more exploring to be done before you zero in on coaching as your career.

Let's begin with bringing out the list you made in the last session on the key skills for a coach.

If you are ready with it start by rating yourself on a scale of 0–10 next to each of the skills according to how you compare yourself with it.

Wrap up your scoring to move on to the next step.

Done?

Now check if you have scored less than 7 on any of the skills.

Yes?

Write these down in a column or mark them clearly. This is to remind you that these are the skills you have to work on and develop them well enough to succeed in the coaching profession.

Reality check

Be true to yourself. There's no point dilly-dallying here if you are not honest with yourself.

Before you get going, ask yourself this:

"Can I build up on the skills where I scored less than 7?"

"Am I committed enough to tackle my weak points and master them?"

You have to be practical at this juncture. The competition out there is cut-throat and scoring less than 7 and not being able to upgrade is not that good a sign.

7.4   Key skills of a coach

Listening –

There is more to listening than just hearing. Capturing the unsaid makes up the core of the listening skill.

Feedback –

Be ready to give some constructive feedback without sounding judgmental.

Observing –

Stay alert to the underlying feelings so you can act on them.

Analyzing –

As a coach you will come across several information which you will have to analyze and draw conclusions from.

Communication –

Be comfortable with communicating yourself, whatever be the medium.

Timing –

Be aware of when your client needs to move to the next stage. You should also know when to ask what type of questions.

Assimilation –

Be prepared by integrating all your information.

Organizing –

If you are not organized, you are bound to get confused. Keep your entire information and work load in an orderly fashion.

Empathy –

Be kind and compassionate to your coachee's needs and problems.

Ethics –

Maintain your coachee's information in confidentiality.

Complimenting –

Feel free to compliment and acknowledge the accomplishments of your coachee whenever necessary. Celebrate successes.

Motivating –

Encourage your coachee's and make them feel confident about what they are doing.

Empowering –

Empower your clients to move ahead and succeed.

Energetic –

You have to be energetic because you need high levels of vigor to be able to motivate.

Positivism –

You as a Personal Coach should be positive in your approach, attitude, tone and even writing. It is your positive outlook that spreads to your coachee's.

Creative –

You have to come up with a number of new ideas to help your coachee. Idea formation plays a major role in the career of a Personal Coach.

Thirst for knowledge –

There are new things happening every minute and you, as a coach, have to be familiar with the changes around you. Update yourself with research and get familiar with new areas that you may encounter. This is so you can help your coachee with what he prefers to work on.

Time to rate yourself again. This time do it with the skills listed above. Now, put together all the skills you scored below 7 for. Remember, you have to work on these. As for those skills where you scored over 7, it's good news! That's half the job done. However, jot down these scores because you have to polish them up. Surely you are a lot closer to understanding your potential as a coach.

On the other hand, let's get more certain on this and take a few more tests, just to be on the safer side.

7.4   Assessment

Rate yourself on the statements below.

And hey! Nobody peeks into this assessment of yours. So, it goes without saying- Be honest!

People come to me for support and guidance. Relations, friends and colleagues turn to me for my opinion and advice on a number of matters.

Strongly Disagree	*Disagree*	*Somewhat Agree*	*Agree*	*Strongly Agree*
1	2	3	4	5

I am willing to put aside my needs and ambitions in the interest of helping others meet their needs and goals.

Strongly Disagree	Disagree	Somewhat Agree	Agree	Strongly Agree
1	2	3	4	5

I can easily build rapport with people I am meeting for the first time.

Strongly Disagree	Disagree	Somewhat Agree	Agree	Strongly Agree
1	2	3	4	5

Every individual is different and I appreciate that. For that reason, I enjoy helping people find their own unique solutions.

Strongly Disagree	Disagree	Somewhat Agree	Agree	Strongly Agree
1	2	3	4	5

People tell me I am a good listener.

Strongly Disagree	Disagree	Somewhat Agree	Agree	Strongly Agree
1	2	3	4	5

I am very particular about standing by my strong sense of values and acting with integrity in both my personal and business life.

Strongly Disagree	Disagree	Somewhat Agree	Agree	Strongly Agree
1	2	3	4	5

I think I have a sixth sense of good intuition.

Strongly Disagree	Disagree	Somewhat Agree	Agree	Strongly Agree
1	2	3	4	5

Though I am not precisely where I want to be in life, I feel fairly balanced and I am consistently working on my own personal growth.

Strongly Disagree	Disagree	Somewhat Agree	Agree	Strongly Agree
1	2	3	4	5

One of the goals on my list is to become an independent coach in my own business.

Strongly Disagree	Disagree	Somewhat Agree	Agree	Strongly Agree
1	2	3	4	5

I am willing to dedicate myself to learn as much as I can about coaching and marketing and I am prepared to invest in myself to receive the proper training and experience.

Strongly Disagree	Disagree	Somewhat Agree	Agree	Strongly Agree
1	2	3	4	5

After you calculate your score for this test, see where you rank in relation to the assessment given below.

A score of 31–50

Bravo! You must be already doing some coaching, right? All you have to do now is make it oficial. This score says that it is time you are paid for the coaching you do. That's how close you are to becoming a professional coach. Good going!

A score of 11–30

You might still be a little hesitant about being a coach. Or, do you just doubt yourself?

Ask yourself. What does your intuition say? Can you see yourself as a coach? Do you fit the bill? Did you land here by chance or because you have a goal to pursue?

Clear your doubts by asking a coach to help you direct your thoughts and give you focus and reason to continue this trail or backtrack.

A score of 0–10

Uh Oh! Looks like coaching is not your cup of tea.

But, fear not. If you still think this is where you want to be then there could be a way out, or should I say 'way in'…

Get yourself a coach. Not only will you gain tremendously from the improvement in the quality of your life, you can also pick up first-hand 'tips and tricks' from your coach on Personal Coaching. Over a period of time, you are sure to decide if coaching is meant for you or not.

8 The key competencies of a Personal Coach

The following competencies are defined by the International Coach Federation. This is what can be expected from a professional coach and what can be observed during a coaching session. In fact, this is what an assessor would listen for during a certification exam.

Setting The Foundation

- Meeting Ethical Guidelines and Professional Standards – Understanding of coaching ethics and standards and ability to apply them appropriately in all coaching situations.
- Understands and exhibits in own behaviors the ICF Standards of Conduct •
Understands and follows all ICF Ethical Guidelines
- Clearly communicates the distinctions between coaching, consulting, psychotherapy and other support professions,
- Refers client to another support professional as needed, knowing when this is needed and the available resources.

Establishing the Coaching Agreement

- Ability to understand what is required in the specific coaching interaction and to come to agreement with the prospective and new client about the coaching process and relationship.
- Understands and effectively discusses with the client the guidelines and specific parameters of the coaching relationship (e.g., logistics, fees, scheduling, inclusion of others if appropriate),
- Reaches agreement about what is appropriate in the relationship and what is not, what is and is not being offered, and about the client's and coach's responsibilities,
- Determines whether there is an effective match between his/her coaching method and the needs of the prospective client.

Co-Creating the Relationship

- Establishing Trust and Intimacy with the Client – Ability to create a safe, supportive environment that produces ongoing mutual respect and trust
- Shows genuine concern for the client's welfare and future,
- Continuously demonstrates personal integrity, honesty and sincerity, •
Establishes clear agreements and keeps promises,
- Demonstrates respect for client's perceptions, learning styles, personal being,

Coaching Presence

- Ability to be fully conscious and create spontaneous relationship with the client, employing a style that is open, flexible and confident
- Is present and flexible during the coaching process, dancing in the moment, •
Accesses own intuition and trusts one's inner knowing – "goes with the gut". • Is
open to not knowing and takes risks,
- Sees many ways to work with the client, and chooses in the moment what is most effective •
Uses humor effectively to create lightness and energy,
- Confidently shifts perspectives and experiments with new possibilities for own action,
- Demonstrates confidence in working with strong emotions, and can self-manage and not be overpowered or enmeshed by client's emotions.

Communicating Effectively

- Active Listening – Ability to focus completely on what the client is saying and is not saying, to understand the meaning of what is said in the context of the client's desires, and to support client self-expression.
- Attends to the client and the client's agenda, and not to the coach's agenda for the client, •
Hears the client's concerns, goals, values and beliefs about what is and is not possible
- Distinguishes between the words, the tone of voice, and the body language,

- Summarizes, paraphrases, reiterates, mirrors back what client has said to ensure clarity and understanding
- Encourages, accepts, explores and reinforces the client's expression of feelings, perceptions, concerns, beliefs, suggestions, etc.,
- Integrates and builds on client's ideas and suggestions,
- Bottom-lines or understands the essence of the client's communication and helps the client get there rather than engaging in long descriptive stories,
- Allows the client to vent or "clear" the situation without judgment or attachment in order to move on to next steps.

Powerful Questioning

- Ability to ask questions that reveal the information needed for maximum benefit to the coaching relationship and the client
- Asks questions that reflect active listening and an understanding of the client's perspective, •
Asks questions that evoke discovery, insight, commitment or action (e.g. those that challenge the client's assumptions),
- Asks open-ended questions that create greater clarity, possibility or new learning,
- Asks questions that move the client towards what they desire, not questions that ask for the client to justify or look backwards.

Direct Communication

- Ability to communicate effectively during coaching sessions, and to use language that has the greatest positive impact on the client
- Is clear, articulate and direct in sharing and providing feedback,
- Reframes and articulates to help the client understand from another perspective what he/she wants or is uncertain about,
- Clearly states coaching objectives, meeting agenda, purpose of techniques or exercises, •
Uses language appropriate and respectful to the client (e.g., non-sexist, non-racist, non-technical, non-jargon),
- Uses metaphor and analogy to help to illustrate a point or paint a verbal picture.

Facilitating Learning and Awareness

- Creating Awareness – Ability to integrate and accurately evaluate multiple sources of information, and to make interpretations that help the client to gain awareness and thereby achieve agreed-upon results
- Goes beyond what is said in assessing client's concerns, not getting hooked by the client's description,
- Invokes inquiry for greater understanding, awareness and clarity,
- Identifies for the client his/her underlying concerns, typical and fixed ways of perceiving himself/herself and the world, differences between the facts and the interpretation, disparities between thoughts, feelings and action,
  - Helps clients to discover for themselves the new thoughts, beliefs, perceptions, emotions, moods, etc. that strengthen their ability to take action and achieve what is important to them,
- Communicates broader perspectives to clients and inspires commitment to shift their viewpoints and find new possibilities for action,
- Helps clients to see the different, interrelated factors that affect them and their behaviors (e.g., thoughts, emotions, body, background),
- Expresses insights to clients in ways that are useful and meaningful for the client,
- Identifies major strengths vs. major areas for learning and growth, and what is most important to address during coaching,
- Asks the client to distinguish between trivial and significant issues, situational vs. recurring behaviors, when detecting a separation between what is being stated and what is being done.

Designing Actions

- Ability to create with the client opportunities for ongoing learning, during coaching and in work/life situations, and for taking new actions that will most effectively lead to agreed-upon coaching results
- Brainstorms and assists the client to define actions that will enable the client to demonstrate, practice and deepen new learning,

- Helps the client to focus on and systematically explore specific concerns and opportunities that are central to agreed-upon coaching goals,
- Engages the client to explore alternative ideas and solutions, to evaluate options, and to make related decisions,
- Promotes active experimentation and self-discovery, where the client applies what has been discussed and learned during sessions immediately afterwards in his/her work or life setting,
- Celebrates client successes and capabilities for future growth,
- Challenges client's assumptions and perspectives to provoke new ideas and find new possibilities for action,
- Advocates or brings forward points of view that are aligned with client goals and, without attachment, engages the client to consider them,
- Helps the client "Do It Now" during the coaching session, providing immediate support, • Encourages stretches and challenges but also a comfortable pace of learning.

Planning and Goal Setting

- Ability to develop and maintain an effective coaching plan with the client
- Consolidates collected information and establishes a coaching plan and development goals with the client that address concerns and major areas for learning and development,
- Creates a plan with results that are attainable, measurable, specific and have target dates,
- Makes plan adjustments as warranted by the coaching process and by changes in the situation, • Helps the client identify and access different resources for learning (e.g., books, other professionals),
- Identifies and targets early successes that are important to the client.

Managing Progress and Accountability

- Ability to hold attention on what is important for the client, and to leave responsibility with the client to take action
- Clearly requests of the client actions that will move the client toward their stated goals, • Demonstrates follow through by asking the client about those actions that the client committed to during the previous session(s),
- Acknowledges the client for what they have done, not done, learned or become aware of since the previous coaching session(s),
- Effectively prepares, organizes and reviews with client information obtained during sessions, • Keeps the client on track between sessions by holding attention on the coaching plan and outcomes, agreed-upon courses of action, and topics for future session(s),
- Focuses on the coaching plan but is also open to adjusting behaviors and actions based on the coaching process and shifts in direction during sessions,

- Is able to move back and forth between the big picture of where the client is heading, setting a context for what is being discussed and where the client wishes to go,
  - Promotes client's self-discipline and holds the client accountable for what they say they are going to do, for the results of an intended action, or for a specific plan with related time frames,
- Develops the client's ability to make decisions, address key concerns, and develop himself/herself (to get feedback, to determine priorities and set the pace of learning, to reflect on and learn from experiences).

Overwhelming isn't it?

Of course I wouldn't expect you to show all these skills during a single coaching session. Look at this list every once in a while and evaluate your coaching session in view of this light.

You'll get there!

9   The key competencies of a Business Coach

In their **Chartered Business Coach** (ChBC ™)credential process, the **Worldwide Association of Business Coaches (WABC)** defined the following Business Coaching Competencies. The business coaching competencies are divided into three areas:

- Self-Management – Knowing Oneself and Self-Mastery •
Core Coaching Skill-base
- Business and Leadership Coaching Capabilities

Reprinted with permission of the Worldwide Association of *Business Coaches*.

Each area includes a listing of competencies. Each competency is illustrated by examples of the behavior expected of a proficient master coach with at least five years of experience.

Newer business coaches are not expected to demonstrate every competency listed here. Rather, the competencies provide a framework against which individuals can map their training and experience. In this way, individual coaches can use the competencies to gauge their progress toward master-level proficiency.

The ChBC designation:

- Sets international standards for senior professional business coaches through a chartered designation, and clearly identifies these standards for buyers of business coaching
- Provides an independent, robust, transparent assessment process that recognizes appropriate levels of education and continuing professional development for the highest standards of professionalism in business coaching
  - Promotes high-caliber leadership in business coaching services for the benefit of clients • Contributes to the definition, development and self-regulation of the business coaching profession

9.1   The Most Advanced Credential for Senior Business Coaches™

The Chartered Business Coach (ChBC) designation is intended for **senior professional business coaches**. It is an international designation that recognizes business coaches who apply their coaching in a variety of contexts, the outcomes of which may be unpredictable. Business coaches at this level are accountable for critical analysis, diagnosis, design, planning, execution and evaluation. They exercise substantial personal autonomy and show significant influence and leadership within their organization, the profession or academic settings.

Chartered status tells the wider community that a business coach has the highest level of specialized subject knowledge and professional competence. The ChBC designation recognizes the experienced practicing business coach who has demonstrated an in-depth knowledge of business coaching, significant personal achievements in the field, professionalism and leadership in the workplace, and a commitment to maintaining expertise through continuing professional development. The ChBC is a stand-alone credential and the highest level of certification.

The ChBC designation can also lead to a fully accredited master's degree. The Master of Arts in Professional Development (Business Coaching) program, offered by the Professional Development Foundation through Middlesex University in the UK, is open to ChBC holders.

10 Self-Management – Knowing Oneself and Self-Mastery

Knowing Yourself – Self-Insight and Understanding

- Having ready access to your thoughts and feelings and being aware of how they affect your behavior
- Be aware of your own emotions and able to recognize what you're feeling at any given time • Know the reasons why you feel the way you do
- Recognize how your feelings affect you and your work performance
- Have a high degree of awareness of what is important to you and the contribution you want to make – your values, purpose and vision
  - Know what you want and go after it •
    Know when your self-talk is helpful
- Know when your self-talk is unhelpful

Acknowledging Your Strengths and Development Needs

a) Having a realistic perception of your strengths and development needs – knowing your strengths and limitations and showing a commitment to continuous learning and self-development
  - Know your strengths and less-developed areas, your abilities and limitations • Reflect on ways to learn from experiences
  - Seek out constructive feedback to improve your performance • Act on constructive feedback to improve your performance
  - Be able to show a sense of humor and perspective about yourself
  - Be a continuous learner: seek opportunities for self-development and lifelong learning, always looking to improve and grow

b) Self-belief – believing in your self-worth and capabilities
  - Present yourself to others as self-assured and confident in your capability
  - Prepare to take an unpopular stand when a decision or strategy compromises your principles
  - Make effective decisions in dificult or ambiguous situations, when time is critical • Trust your instincts and hunches, even in uncertain situations
  - Emphasize your strengths and appreciate them; accept your shortcomings and make allowances for them

Self-Mastery – Managing Your Thoughts, Feelings and Behaviors in Ways that Promote Behavior Contributing to Career and Organization Success

a) Self-regulation – managing your reactions and emotions constructively

Monitor and contain distressing emotions and regulate them so they don't keep you from doing the things you need to do

- Maintain self-control under adverse or stressful conditions (e.g., maintain demeanor, composure and temperament)
- Manage your own behavior to prevent or reduce feelings of stress •

Be able to think clearly and to stay focused when under pressure •

Accept negative feedback without becoming defensive

- Talk yourself out of a bad mood
- Distinguish between a client's contribution, and your own contribution, to your emotional reactions

b) Integrity – choosing ethical courses of action and being steadfast in your principles and beliefs

- Set an example by consistently modeling high standards of honesty and integrity •
Confront unethical behavior conducted by others
- Be willing to admit to mistakes, even in the face of adverse consequences •
Build trust by demonstrating ethical behavior
- Take responsibility for your failures and mistakes, without blaming others or the circumstances

c) Self-responsibility – assuming personal responsibility and accountability for your performance

- Assume personal accountability for meeting goals, outcomes and deadlines •
Follow through on projects, dificulties and inquiries to full resolution
- Plan and organize work effectively
- Do whatever it takes (within reason) to meet commitments •
Keep your promises and fulfill your commitments

d) Adaptability – flexibility in handling change

- Take changing priorities and new developments in your stride, even in the face of ambiguity
- Be flexible and adaptable when confronted with unexpected changes •
Modify an approach or strategy as situations change
- Be willing to modify a strongly held position in the face of contrary evidence •
Adjust to new situations easily
- Effectively juggle multiple demands on your time

e) Emphasizing excellence – setting for yourself, and confidently pursuing, challenging goals and high standards

- Set yourself challenging goals
- Maintain commitment to goals in the face of obstacles and frustrations •
Demonstrate a willingness to take calculated risks
- Remain optimistic and persistent, even in the face of setbacks or disappointments •
Be confident that you will find a solution when you are under pressure
- Constantly seek ways to improve your performance
- Operate from hope of success rather than fear of failure •
Feel capable of exerting influence on your life situation

f) Initiative – taking independent action to change the direction of events

- Show inclination to initiate rather than react
- Aim to achieve more than is required or expected of you •

Bend the rules when necessary to get the job done

- Take anticipatory action to avoid problems before they happen •

Independently seek out and act on opportunities

g) Creativity and innovation – being receptive to new ideas and being able to generate alternative ways to view and define problems

- Seek out innovative approaches and current developments related to your area of expertise
- Seek out new ideas and approaches from a wide variety of sources
- Experiment with different and novel ways to deal with problems and opportunities •

See alternative ways to view and define problems

- Think up alternative solutions to problems and challenges

11 Core Coaching Skill-Base

Creating the Foundations for Business Coaching

    a) Working within established ethical guidelines and professional standards

- Abide by the ethical guidelines, standards and code of conduct of your own professional association and others
- Clearly communicate the distinctions between coaching and other types of helping relationships, such as mentoring, counseling/psychotherapy and consulting
- Recognize the limits of your own competence, and refer to other professionals when appropriate

    b) Agreeing on a clear and effective contract for the coaching relationship

- Develop a working agreement on the nature of the coach-client relationship (e.g., roles, responsibilities and boundaries)
- Establish a formal coaching agreement/contract (either written or oral) that is specific, fair and effective, and that reflects the organizational context
- Agree on terms of confidentiality
- Determine whether there is an appropriate match between your own background and coaching style and the prospective client's needs and expectations
- Have a clear policy on note-keeping and/or taping sessions (e.g., for supervision purposes) and communicate this to the client

Developing the Business Coaching Relationship

    a) Establishing trust and respect

- Demonstrate a genuine concern for the client's welfare and success •
Demonstrate a strong belief in the boundless potential of others
- Consistently work to establish trust and honest communication with the client •
Establish clear agreements and keep promises
- Clearly and candidly share your values, attitudes, beliefs and emotions when appropriate •
Encourage the client to take on new and challenging tasks, while providing appropriate support
- Create an environment of safety and security when dealing with sensitive issues
- Create an environment of safety and security in which the client is able to share all sides of him/herself (e.g., his/her ambitions, needs and fears)
- Be honest and truthful in dificult situations (e.g., prepared to tell the client what he/she needs to hear but others won't say)

b) Establishing rapport
- Have an open and responsive presence
- Be comfortable sharing your intuitions with the client
- Demonstrate a willingness to take risks and to enter the unknown
- Have a very flexible approach to coaching and be able to adapt your style to what works best for the client
- Make appropriate use of humor to make the work more fun
- Be able to tolerate open expression of strong emotions directed at you without becoming defensive
- Be able to manage the client's expression of strong emotions about his/her situation without getting caught up in the client's emotions
- Be able to work with a variety of learning styles in individuals •

Give objective feedback in a non-judgmental manner

Promoting Client Understanding

a) Listening to understand
- Adjust easily to the client's agenda
- Hear the client's expectations about what is and is not possible
- Confirm understanding by observing and interpreting non-verbal signals (e.g., body language, facial expressions, tone of voice, etc.)
- Use positive body language and non-verbal signals to demonstrate openness and undivided attention
- Demonstrate active listening by seeking clarification, rephrasing the client's statements and summarizing to check understanding
- Encourage the client to "say more" – create a positive climate for the client to express his/ her feelings, perceptions, concerns, suggestions, etc.
- Acknowledge the client's ideas and suggestions and build on them in discussions
- Offer non-judgmental responses that encourage the client to explore and validate his/her feelings, concerns and aspirations
- Use silence as an appropriate intervention to elicit more information •

Listen to the client's emotional undercurrents
- Pay attention to what the client isn't saying about issues discussed

b) Questioning effectively
- Ask questions that reflect an understanding of the client's point of view •

Ask challenging questions that help the client to self-discover
- Pose open-ended questions that help the client to clarify issues
- Ask questions that help the client to develop new perspectives and new possibilities for action and learning
- Ask questions that evoke commitment to action
- Ask questions that steer the client towards his/her desired outcomes

c) Communicating clearly
- Prepare in advance for the coaching session
- Ensure that feedback to the client is clear and meaningful in terms of the client's intended outcomes
- Present alternative ways of viewing the client's situation that are useful and meaningful to the client
- Clearly state the coaching objectives, and the rationale for using particular techniques or exercises
- Use language appropriate and respectful to the client (e.g., non-sexist, non-racist, non-technical, non-jargon)
- Use analogies, metaphors and examples to help the client grasp an idea
- Clarify and review with the client the information obtained during sessions

d) Facilitating depth of understanding
- Understand and respond to the client's unspoken feelings and concerns
- Identify patterns and discrepancies in the client's thoughts and/or behaviors
- Enable the client to discover the thoughts, feelings and behaviors that will help him/her to achieve meaningful outcomes
- Add order, clarity, depth of understanding and perspective to problematic situations •
Help the client to look at the broader context of issues or problems

- Create an environment that supports exploration and change
- Help the client to recognize the impact of his/her thoughts and feelings on behavior • Recognize the client's strengths and areas for learning and growth
- Help the client to identify the most important issues to address during coaching • Contribute your knowledge, experience and expertise without giving advice
- Employ a variety of perspectives when trying to make sense of a situation

Facilitating the Personal Transformation

a) Promoting action

- Help the client to identify actions that will enable him/her to demonstrate and strengthen new learning
- Encourage the client to think deeply and creatively, to look for new or different approaches to take
- Help the client to systematically evaluate identified concerns, options and opportunities • Encourage the client to make appropriate decisions after exploring possible outcomes
- Ensure that the coaching session leaves the client feeling motivated to apply what was learned in his/her life setting
- Recognize and celebrate the client's successes
- Encourage and support the client to apply new knowledge or skills immediately (i.e., during the coaching session)
- Help the client to determine a challenging yet realistic pace of learning

b) Focusing on goals

- Work with the client to develop a coaching plan and goals for development
- Encourage the client to keep focused on concerns and opportunities relevant to agreed-upon goals
- Ensure that the coaching plan and development goals address the client's concerns and major areas for learning and development
- Create development goals that are specific, measurable, action-oriented and results-oriented, and that have an appropriate time frame
- Assess coaching progress and adjust goals based on interim results and changing priorities
- Help the client to evaluate and access the learning resources (e.g., people, books, courses) that will support his/her desired outcomes
- Help the client to focus and build on his/her successes

c) Building resiliency
- Help the client to remain on track between sessions (e.g., to take the actions needed to accomplish his/her goals)
- Spend time in subsequent sessions checking the client's progress regarding actions committed to previously
- Acknowledge what the client has and has not done, learned and become aware of since the previous session
- Positively confront the client when he/she does not take agreed-upon actions • Effectively relate what is being discussed to where the client wants to be
- Promote self-discipline in the client by holding the client responsible and accountable for agreed-upon actions
- Develop the client's ability to coach him/herself

d) Managing termination of coaching
- Assess the client's readiness for termination of coaching
- Take whatever steps are necessary to ensure that the client can continue his/her development • Clarify with the client any follow-up arrangements
- Guide the client and other stakeholders in devising a long-range development plan
- Recommend internal and external means of development that best fit the needs of the client and the organization
- Communicate with the client's manager or other stakeholders to ensure commitment to the client's future development, including regular progress reviews
- Make yourself available for questions and clarification after the coaching ends
- Check in with the client occasionally, as appropriate, to maintain the relationship

Professional Development

a) Maintaining and improving professional skills
- Regularly seek out client feedback on your performance to help you develop your practice • Recognize your own limitations as a coach and seek supervision when appropriate
- Use supervision on a regular basis to maintain and improve your coaching skills
- Consult with supervisors and colleagues regarding client and coaching issues and issues related to your own professional development as a coach
- Attend conferences and workshops to develop your coaching skills, expertise and knowledge • Read books, journals and articles to keep abreast of current developments in coaching

12 Business and Leadership Coaching Capabilities

Alignment

a) Understanding the business and displaying a strong grounding in business knowledge and competencies

- Bring to the coaching situation a wide range of relevant knowledge about, and experience in, large corporations
- Bring to the coaching situation a wide range of relevant knowledge about, and experience in, SMEs and start-up/entrepreneurial businesses
- Understand the broader business context in which the client operates (e.g., market outlook, competition, products and services, clients and customers)
- Become familiar with the vision, goals and objectives of the organization and its stakeholders • Understand the organization's practices and policies as they relate to achieving business objectives
- Understand how the organization evaluates the client's performance and results
- Understand the client's role and position relative to the organization's overall mission, strategy, and key business initiatives
- Become familiar with the organization's human resource policies and procedures (e.g., on sensitive issues such as sexual harassment, diversity and incident reporting)
- Become aware of how decisions are made and implemented within the organization (e.g., corporate governance principles, structures and channels for conducting business)

b) Demonstrating proficiency in systems thinking

- Be equally comfortable discussing broad conceptual issues and specific practical issues • Encourage the client to look at the wider picture
- Help the client to see his/her position and the organization through various viewpoints and perspectives
- Apply a systems perspective to identify wider patterns of activity (internal and external) that help or hinder achievement
- Recognize the client's interdependence with other people and processes in the organization
- Identify patterns or meanings in events and data that are not obviously connected
- Identify parallels between the dynamics in the coaching relationship and the client's impact on people and processes in the organization
- Approach each problem situation with a clear perception of the political reality
- Be comfortable coaching in a turbulent and constantly changing business system, filled with ambiguity

c) Aligning coaching initiatives with the business
  • Identify and set coaching and development priorities within the context of business plans •
Ensure that coaching is primarily concerned with the client's development in the context
    of organizational needs
  • Be clear about the responsibility of the client and other stakeholders to take action
  • Challenge the client, when necessary, to relate his/her behavior back to company aims •
Strive to maximize the client's contribution to the organization's needs
  • Be flexible in adapting the client's development needs to changing business priorities
  • Be able to ask tough, challenging questions that make the client think along new strategic
    lines
  • Be comfortable coaching around international issues and agendas

Leadership Knowledge and Credibility

a) Acting as a strong and influential role model
  • Be able to inspire and motivate others at the highest levels
  • Help the client to create and communicate a compelling and inspirational picture of the
    future
  • Model and demonstrate leadership behaviors in ways that enable the client to enact these
    behaviors for him/herself
  • Practice leadership and integrate leadership qualities and behaviors into your working practice

b) Possessing thorough working knowledge of the world of the executive leader and leadership development
  - Know how leaders learn and the processes that facilitate leadership learning •
  Understand the challenges of effective leadership
  - Be thoroughly familiar with the demands faced by leaders in their particular business •
  Identify appropriate leadership development processes
  - Identify and select coaching techniques appropriate to the client's leadership developmental tasks
  - Identify and articulate the difference between a manager and a leader •
  Facilitate the client's transition from manager to leader
  - Understand and communicate the qualities required for effective leadership

c) Displaying highly developed communication and interpersonal competencies •
  Display a high level of confidence in working within the leadership arena •
  Discuss issues in a language appropriate to the business context
  - Understand the points of influence within the organization •
  Work beneath the strong ego of the leader
  - Challenge the leader to raise standards in all areas

Coach as Leader and Developer of Own Business

a) Creating and managing business relationship networks •
  Be able to win new clients
  - Be able to generate referrals from other professionals
  - Be able to generate new business through word of mouth
  - Provide the organization and the client with background information about yourself and your practice (e.g., references, fees and business practices)
  - Maintain a large network of contacts with other qualified professionals •
  Refer clients when you are not the best possible resource

b) Collaborating with other coaches
  - Establish alliances with other coaches to enable delivery of large contracts •
  Identify and develop resources and referrals
  - Share values and ethics with other coaches •
  Share best practices with other coaches
  - Promote the coaching profession
  - Learn about and develop the coaching profession

c) Developing yourself in a business capacity
- Attend events (e.g., workshops and conferences) to develop your understanding of leadership and business ideas
- Read professional books and trade journals (e.g., Harvard Business Review) to keep up with business developments
- Read business newspapers (e.g., Financial Times) and business pages to stay informed about business and economic conditions

Creating and Maintaining Partnerships with all Stakeholders in the Business Coaching Process

- Proactively develop a network of relationships and strategic partnerships within the organization, and maintain it through regular contact and follow-up
- Understand and effectively discuss with the client and decision-maker the guidelines and parameters of the coaching contract (e.g., logistics, fees, inclusion of others if appropriate)
- Recognize and involve Human Resources and other stakeholders as appropriate when agreeing on accountability
- Understand the needs and requirements of the coaching sponsor
- Participate in the organization's process for selecting, matching and orienting business coaches •
Develop a formal written confidentiality agreement before the coaching begins (e.g., specify which information will and will not be shared, in which circumstances, with whom and how)

- Communicate openly about coaching progress with the client and other stakeholders (within the limits of the agreed-upon confidentiality)
- Facilitate communication between the client and the organization about what the client is working on, his/her progress and his/her support needs
- Abide by the organization's values, ethical practices, confidentiality agreements, business practices and human resource policies; withdraw if these are incompatible with your own values

Understanding Organizational Behavior and Organizational Development Principles

- Understand organizational processes and how to improve their eficiency and effectiveness • Analyze the elements, principles and relationships in organizational structure, culture and change management
- Know how to facilitate the creation of vision and the clarification of direction
- Know how to facilitate the development and implementation of strategic and operational plans
- Know how to facilitate the development of strategies for leading and managing organizational change

Assessment

a) Assessing the client
  - Select from a wide variety of assessment instruments (e.g., 360-degree feedback and measures of personality, learning styles, interests, leadership style)
  - Carry out additional assessments of variables such as the organizational culture, team communication, organizational trust, quality, employee satisfaction, eficiency and profitability
  - Administer only those instruments for which you have been fully trained, certified or otherwise prepared
  - Explain clearly the strengths and limitations of assessment instruments •
  Maintain the client's confidentiality by protecting assessment data
  - Provide a safe, supportive environment in which to deliver assessment feedback •
  Deliver feedback in ways that encourage the client to act upon the assessment
  - Help the client to use assessment data to create a development action plan

b) Assessing the individual and organizational benefits of business coaching •
  Know how to measure the effectiveness of coaching
  - Demonstrate commitment to measuring coaching success
  - Create relevant return on investment (or other models) for identifying added value
  - Use pre- or post-coaching assessments (e.g., 360-degree feedback) to measure results •
  Offer reliable and valid means for measuring the results and outcomes of coaching
  - Establish goals in the contracting phase so that the performance of both you and the client can be measured

Having Respect for and Knowledge about Multicultural Issues and Diversity

- Adapt the language and/or approach you use during coaching to racial and cultural differences •
Be aware of how cultural dynamics influence business processes, interactions and outcomes •
Help to form effective strategies consistent with the organization's position in a global economy •
Help the client to recognize the value of diversity, and to maximize the benefits of racial and
    cultural differences in ways that improve outcomes
- Demonstrate personal commitment to treating people equally and with respect and dignity •
Clearly understand the business benefits of effectively managing racial and cultural diversity •
Understand potential preferences and biases associated with your own racial and cultural
    identity, and how these might enhance or impede your delivery of services

And there you have it. Just show the above described competencies during your coaching sessions and some day you might become a WABC Chartered Business Coach™ like me!

Overwhelmed? You should be :-)

Coaching is not just having great conversations. It takes a lot more to become a Master Certified Coach whether it is as a Personal Coach or as a Business Coach. But keep in mind that every great journey starts with the first step....

Describing these competencies is not to scare you off but to show you what you need to focus on as a coach.

So, you just keep on walking and enjoy every step of the way while you learn to become the best coach you can be!